Constitutional Law

A BRIEF SYNOPSIS OF Constitutional Law, book formation

Format for notes.

Constitutional Law

The Changing Powers of the Federal Government

When cases which raise

Constitution question are appealed from the lower courts decisions.

The courts decisions in these cases result in federal government's powers

Being enlarged , reduced, clarified, or reinforced.

A Brief Overview of The

CONSTITUTION

The Constitution is divided into seven articles

Article I   how the legislative branch is organized, power and duties   the senate and house representatives.

Article II executive powers and duties given to the office of the President of the United States.

Article III creates power of the Supreme Court, and delegates to congress the power to

Establish lower federal courts.

Article IV regulates the relationships between the federal government and the states.

Article V declares the constitution to be "the supreme n law of the land".

Article VII specifies that nine of the thirteen states had to ratify the constitution for it to Become effective.

Supreme Court Opinions

The supreme court writes more than 150 opinions pre year.

Plus an explanation of the legal principles which is how the courts reaches a decision.

The supreme court will not decide every case that is brought to its attention.

A supreme court decision must have the agreement of the majority of the justices.

The chief justices will then call for a vote.

One of the justic3es will be assigned to write a majority opinion.

Principles may be changed by Supreme Court or by constitutional amendments.

The greatest number of justices sign a plurality. Keep in mind that

Plurality opinion not provide authoritative statements of the law.

Understanding the Brief of an Opinion

A paralegal may be asked to brief court opinion for an attorney.

The seven parts of a brief, including the:

Facts of the case what situation prompted this case to arise.

2. Judicial history

3 Issue

4. Holding

5. Reason

6. Procedural Consequences

7. Subsequent Judicial history.

No state shall make or enforce any law which

Shall abridge the privileges or immunities

Of 5the citizens of the United States

Nor shall any state deprive any person

Of life, liberty, or property, without due process of la.

Criminal Procedures

Decency, security, and liberty must be observed.

Always a good case to reference to   Olmstead v. United States, 277 U.S. 438 (1928)

Two more important cases to remember Mapp v. Ohio

And Gideon v. Wain-Wright

Exclusionary Rule

Remember that the exclusionary rule

Is based on the Fourth Amendments protection

Against the unreasonable searches and seizures.

Right to Counsel

This is the Sixth Amendment.

Remember that the Fourteenth Amendment does not incorporate

Guarantees " the due process" found in the Sixth Amendment " fundamental right".

Equal protection of Law

A good case that we all should know, Brown v. Board of Education of Topeka.

Commerce Clause

Look up Article I, Section 8, clause 3 of the Constitution "THE COMMERCE CLAUSE"

Page formation : this book is format for notes on all pages.